This book belongs to

_____

It was given to me by

_____

On

_____

My Bedtime Bible Prayers

Published in 2019 by Kregel Children's Books,
an imprint of Kregel Publications, 2450 Oak
Industrial Dr. NE, Grand Rapids, MI 49505 USA

1st edition, 1st print
Copyright © Scandinavia Publishing House 2018
info@sph.as | www.sph.as
Illustrations by Gavin Scott
Text by Karoline Pahus Pedersen
Cover design & book layout by
Gao Hanyu

ISBN 978-0-8254-4633-7
Printed in China

My Bedtime
Bible Prayers

KREGEL
CHILDREN'S BOOKS

Contents

MAKE A DIFFERENCE

Don't look out only for your own interests, but take an interest in others, too.

Philippians 2:4 NLT

John 6:1–14

Dear God,
Will You help me look
out for other people and
not only think about myself
and what I want?
Let me help someone who
needs a smile or a hug.
Good night, God!
Amen.

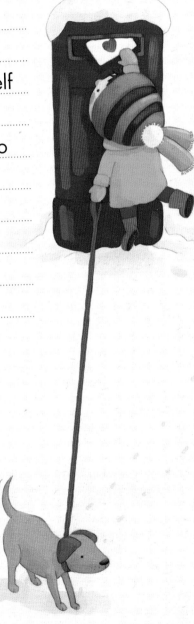

Who is one
person you can
do something kind
for tomorrow?

My heart is filled with joy. I burst out in songs of thanksgiving.

Psalm 28:7 NLT

2 Samuel 22:1–4

God in heaven,
Thank You for all the good things in my life, like jumping around and singing songs and being happy.
I am Your child, and that makes me a child of the God who is always there!
Good night, God!
Amen.

Name one thing that happened today that you are grateful for.

QUITE BLESSED

I will bless you with plenty of food and water and keep you strong.

Exodus 23:25

Matthew 6:25–27

Hi God,
Thank You for creating
yummy food for me to eat.
I'm glad You care if I have
everything I need for my
body to be healthy and to
keep me growing.
I'm quite blessed!
Night-night, Dad in heaven!
Amen.

What is one of
your favorite
foods?

GOD IS WITH US

God loved the people of this world so much that he gave his only Son, so that everyone who has faith in him will have eternal life.

John 3:16

John 15:15

Dear God,
Thanks for sending Jesus to live among us so we can become friends with You and be with You forever.
I pray that my faith and my friendship with You will grow stronger.
Good night, God!
Amen.

How can you spend more time with Jesus and get to know Him better?

MY GOD CREATED THE SKIES

I often think of the heavens your hands have made, and of the moon and stars you put in place.

Psalm 8:3

Genesis 1:14–19

Dear Dad in heaven,
It's amazing how You make new beautiful skies every day.
Thanks for giving me hands so I can play and create things, too!
Good night, God.
Amen.

How do you like to use your hands?

GOD KNOWS ME

Even the hairs on your head are counted.

Luke 12:7

Psalm 139:15–16

Dear God in heaven,
It amazes me to think about how well You know me—
even how many hairs are on my head!
I want to be good at seeing things about You, about
other people, and about myself, too.
Good night, God!
Amen.

What is something special
you know about a family
member or a close friend?

ALL CHILDREN ARE WELCOME

Let the children come to me! Don't try to stop them. People who are like these children belong to God's Kingdom.

Luke 18:16

Matthew 18:1–5

Dear God,
Thank You that all children
can come to You.
We never interrupt You, and
You don't mind if we are silly,
noisy, or sit on the dresser.
I pray that nothing will ever
stop me from being close to
You.
Night-night, Dad!
Amen.

Did you know God never sleeps (Psalm 121:3)? You can always come and talk to Him!

You let me rest in fields of green gras
You lead me to streams of peaceful
water, and you refresh my life.

Psalm 23:2–3

Matthew 11:28–30

Dear Dad,

I love to relax and talk to You.

Thanks for always spending time with me and listening to me.

Please help my parents to find time to relax, too!

Good night, God!

Amen.

Did you know that God relaxed on the seventh day after creating the world?

I WILL SHARE MY SMILE

A friendly smile makes you happy, and good news makes you feel strong.

Proverbs 15:30

Genesis 21:5–7

Hi Dad,
Thanks for giving me my smile. It looks good on me.
Help me share my smile with the people I meet tomorrow, even those who haven't put their smile on.
Night-night, Dad!
Amen.

Who do you think would like a smile from you tomorrow?

I'M ALWAYS LOVED

I am sure that nothing can separate us from God's love.

Romans 8:38

Matthew 28:19–20

Dear God,
I am so glad Your love for
me never stops.
When I am sad or hurt,
You are there with me.
Even when I have been
unkind or mean to
someone, You forgive me
and love me.
Help me know Your love
better each day.
Good night, God!
Amen.

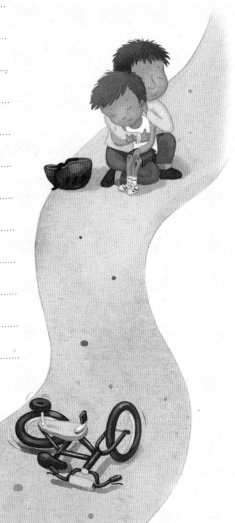

How can you show
love to someone?

MAY WE CHOOSE YOU

As for me and my family, we will serve the LORD.

Joshua 24:15 NLT

Genesis 12:1–8

Dear Dad in heaven,
Thanks for my family. Each one of them means something very special to me.
I pray that we may all choose to live like Jesus and spend our lives together with You.
Good night, God!
Amen.

How do you like to spend time with your family?

GOD IS IN CONTROL

Your word is a lamp
that gives light
wherever I walk.

Psalm 119:105

Psalm 23:4

Hi Dad,
Thank You for showing me how I should live and what I should do. I want to always follow You! You are in charge of my life. I will trust You to take good care of me because You love me. Night-night, Dad! Amen.

What have you learned from the Bible about how to treat others and yourself?

FOREVER—FOR REAL!

Eternal life is to know you,
the only true God, and to know
Jesus Christ, the one you sent.

John 17:3

Luke 2:8–20

Dear God in heaven,

How awesome it is that my life with You is forever!

Thanks for sending Jesus to be my special friend.

I am excited to spend so much time with You. I want

to know all about who You are—the only true God!

Good night, God.

Amen.

Do you know Jesus? If not, you can ask Him to forgive you for the wrong things you have done and accept His offer to be friends forever.

AT THE TOP OF MY LUNGS

Let everything that has breath praise the LORD.

Psalm 150:6 NIV

2 Samuel 6:12–15

Dear God,
I love singing and playing
songs about You and how
great You are.
You are the best, the
wisest—and You are God
over the whole entire earth!
Good night, God!
Amen.

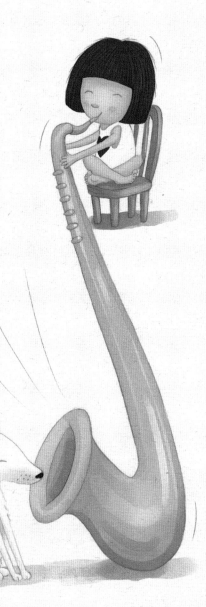

What is your
favorite song to sing
to God?

PEACEFUL SLEEP

In peace I will lie down and sleep, for you alone, O LORD, will keep me safe.

Psalm 4:8 NLT

Psalm 121:4–6

Hi Dad,
Thanks for my stuffed animals, my pillow, and my bed.
I'm going to fall asleep soon.
I'm glad that You never sleep, and You are always by my side.
Help me to know Your peace and to have a good night's rest.
Good night, God!
Amen.

If you wake up in the night, what can you do to remind yourself that God is with you?

BE THE BEST ME

Whatever you do, do it all for the glory of God.

1 Corinthians 10:31 NLT

1 Samuel 16:7

Dear God in heaven,

I'm glad it's not just the big things that count, but also the little acts of kindness and friendship. I can bring You glory on the playground and at the dinner table, too!

Help me do my very best, even when it feels like no one sees it.

Good night, God!

Amen.

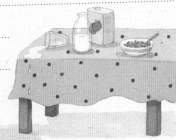

What is one thing you can do tomorrow to bring a smile to God's face?

GOD IS HERE TO HELP

I am the LORD your God. I am holding your hand, so don't be afraid. I am here to help you.

Isaiah 41:13

Daniel 3

Dear Dad,

Thanks for being with me no matter what I go through.

Even when I feel worried or afraid, remind me that

You are close to me and love me.

You are my God, and I will put my trust in You.

Good night, God!

Amen.

What makes you feel better when you are afraid or worried?

GOD IS FAITHFUL

It is wonderful each morning to tell about your love and at night to announce how faithful you are.

Psalm 92:2

Psalm 136:1–9

Dear God,

Thank You for being faithful to me.

Every morning You make the sun rise to give us light and warmth.

Every day You give us life, breath, family, friends, and laughter.

Every day and every night, I can trust You to be You.

Night-night, God!

Amen.

Who can you count on to be there for you when you need them?

GOD KNOWS MY NAME

I have called you by name; you are mine.

Isaiah 43:1 NLT

Psalm 139:1–6

Dear Dad in heaven,
Thank You that You made
me and know everything
about me.
I belong to You, like a child
belongs to their mom and
dad. Thanks for keeping me
close and loving me.
My life is in Your hands—and
that's such a good thing!
Good night, God!
Amen.

Did you know God always
wants what is best for you
(Matthew 7:9-11)?

If you love each other, everyone will know that you are my disciples.

John 13:35

Philippians 2:3

Hi Dad,

Thanks for my friends—I love having fun with them!

Please help me to be kind and helpful when we play so they will know how much I like them.

I want to be just like You when I grow up.

Good night, God!

Amen.

How can you show your friends that you love them?

SWEET DREAMS

When you lie down, you will not be afraid; when you lie down, your sleep will be sweet.

Proverbs 3:24 NIV

Psalm 139:7–12

Dear God in heaven,

Thanks for being close by while I sleep.

It's amazing that You can be in heaven and here

right beside me—all at the same time!

Good night, God!

Amen.

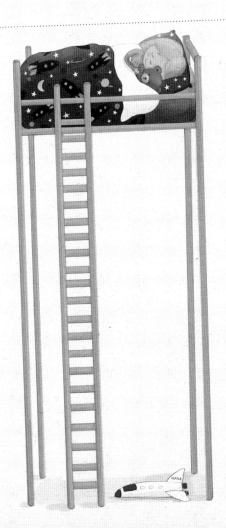

What makes you feel cozy and ready for sleep at night?

I ENJOY MY TALENTS

In his grace, God has given us different gifts for doing certain things well.

Romans 12:6 NLT

1 Timothy 4:14–15

Hi Dad,

I love making up new games. Thank You for giving me an active imagination.

Help me not to brag when I'm good at one thing and my friends are good at something else. Instead, help us all to use our gifts for others.

Good night, God!

Amen.

What are you really good at?

CHOOSE GOODNESS

Do not forget to do good and to share with others.

Hebrews 13:16 NIV

John 13:34

Dear God,
When someone hurts me
or my friend, will You
please help me not to be
mean back?
Help me to be brave and
to stand up for people
when they are not treated
fairly.
Please let me know what
to say.
Good night, God!
Amen.

What is a good thing to say or
do when someone is being mean
to you or to someone else?

GIVE GOD YOUR WORRIES

God cares for you, so turn all your worries over to him.

1 Peter 5:7

Luke 7:11–17

Dear God in heaven,
Thanks that I can ask You for help when I have a
problem, big or small.
I'm glad You care about me and my problems, even
when things don't turn out the way I want.
Good night, God!
Amen.

What is one thing
you needed help with
today?

A FOLLOWER OF GOD

If you keep on obeying
what I have said, you
truly are my disciples.

John 8:31

Matthew 5:14–16

Dear Dad,
Thank You for talking to
me through the Bible. It has
so many amazing stories!
The Bible tells me You are
full of joy, kindness, and
patience.
I want to follow You and be
just like You.
Good night, God!
Amen.

What stories from the
Bible do you know?

GOD CAN DO ANYTHING

There are some things that people cannot do, but God can do anything.

Matthew 19:26

Matthew 28:1–10

Hi Dad,

How great is it that nothing is impossible for You! You are so wise and strong.

There are lots of things I can't do or need help doing.

Please share Your wisdom and strength with me when things are hard or scary.

Good night, God!

Amen.

What is one thing that is impossible for you to do alone?

I AM BRAVE

Be strong and brave!

2 Samuel 2:7 NIV

1 Samuel 17:34–37

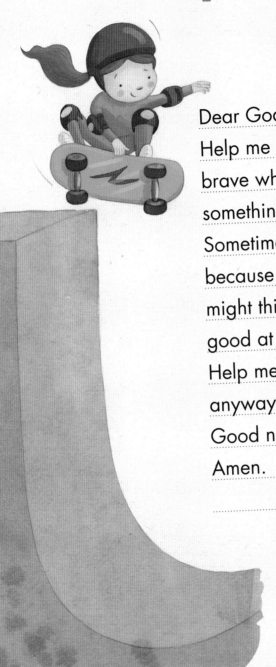

Dear God in heaven,
Help me to be strong and
brave when I am doing
something hard.
Sometimes I'm scared
because other people
might think I'm not very
good at something.
Help me to do my best
anyway and trust in You.
Good night, God!
Amen.

What is one thing you
would like to do that
takes a lot of courage?

I AM A BLESSING

Treat others just as you want to be treated.

Luke 6:31

1 Samuel 18:1–3

Dear God,
Thank You for showing me
how to treat everyone I
know and meet.
Help me to pay attention
when someone needs a
friend, needs help, or needs
to be alone for a while.
I want to treat others with
kindness just as I want to be
treated with kindness.
Good night, God!
Amen.

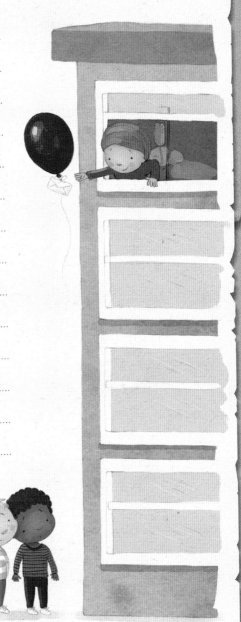

What does it mean to
treat someone kindly?

I have been given all authority in heaven and on earth!

Matthew 28:18

Mark 4:35–41

Dear God,

It's amazing that You are the most powerful person who has ever existed. There is no one stronger or greater than You.

I'm so glad that You love me and that You are my friend. You are my hero!

Good night, God.

Amen.

What is one thing you are glad God can do that no one else can do?

I WILL BE TRUTHFUL

Giving an honest answer is a sign of true friendship.

Proverbs 24:26

Colossians 3:8–10

Dear Dad in heaven,
Sometimes it seems easier not to tell the truth when I feel bad or don't want to get in trouble.
Please forgive me, and help me to tell the truth, especially when it's hard.
Thank You for loving me even when I mess up.
Good night, God!

Amen.

What does it mean to be honest?

GOD KNOWS WHAT I NEED

Your Father knows what you need before you ask.

Matthew 6:8

Luke 11:9–13

Dear God in heaven,
Thanks for always hearing
my prayers and knowing
what I need.
I'm glad that I can ask You
about anything—even
stuff that feels scary or
uncomfortable.
Good night, God!
Amen.

What is one thing you got
recently that made you
happy?

MADE BY GOD

You are the one who put me together inside my mother's body, and I praise you because of the wonderful way you created me.

Psalm 139:13–14

Jeremiah 1:5

Hi Dad,

It is amazing to think that You formed me when I was inside my mother's belly. In fact, I'm still being made: a new tooth is growing in my mouth.

I really like me—thanks for making me so well!

Good night, God!

Amen.

What is one thing you like about yourself?

THE LORD'S PRAYER

Our Father in heaven,
help us to honor
your name.
Come and set up
your kingdom,
so that everyone on earth
will obey you,
as you are obeyed
in heaven.
Give us our food for today.
Forgive us for doing wrong,
as we forgive others.
Keep us from being tempted
and protect us from evil.

Matthew 6:9–13

Put up with each other, and forgive anyone who does you wrong, just as Christ has forgiven you.

Colossians 3:13

Romans 4:25

Dear God in heaven,
Thank You for loving me
when I'm feeling upset.
It's awful when my toys
break—especially when
someone else breaks them.
Please help me to forgive
them as You forgive me
when I do wrong.
Good night, God!
Amen.

Has anyone broken some
of your toys? What did
you do?

GOD'S PLANS ARE GOOD

Your kindness and love
will always be with me
each day of my life.

Psalm 23:6

Jeremiah 29:11

Dear Dad,

You are such a good God. Thank You for having plans for my future that are full of Your kindness, love, and hope.

I pray that all my friends will also know what a good God You are.

Good night, God!

Amen.

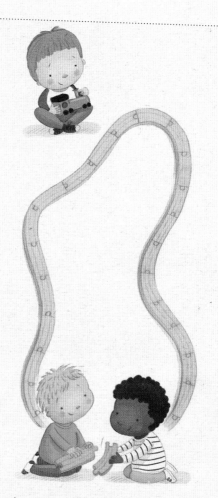

What is one good thing that God has done for you or your family?

GOD COMES ALONG WITH ME

Don't be afraid, for I am with you.
Don't be discouraged, for I am your
God. I will strengthen you and help yo

Isaiah 41:10 NLT

Daniel 6:21–23

Dear God,
I can get shy when I go to new places where there are people I don't know.
Please help me to be myself and know that Your peace goes with me no matter where I am.
Good night, God!
Amen.

How can you tell when you are feeling shy or uncomfortable?

GOD IS GOOD

The Lord has been good to me.

Psalm 116:7 NLT

Matthew 9:27–31

Hi Dad,
Thank You that I have
everything I need—and
even more than I need!
You are so good to me.
Help me to get better at
seeing all the ways You are
good to me each and every
day.
Good night, God!
Amen.

What is one thing you
can thank God for
today?

TRUTHS ABOUT GOD

The Spirit will make you wise and let you understand what it means to know God.

Ephesians 1:17

John 14:26

Dear God in heaven,
There are so many
things about You that I
don't know yet.
Please fill me with Your
Spirit so I can know You
better.
Good night, God!
Amen.

How do you think
you can get to know
God better?

IT PAYS OFF

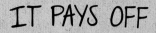

Be strong and do not give up, for your work will be rewarded.

2 Chronicles 15:7 NIV

Luke 10:25–37

Dear God,
Sometimes helping people can feel like a bother.
But it makes You happy when we take care of each
other, so teach me not to give up on being kind and
helpful to those around me.
Good night, God!
Amen.

What is one thing you
can do tomorrow to
help someone?

A GOD WHO LOVES

We love because God loved us first.

1 John 4:19

Romans 13:8–10

Hi Dad,

It's wonderful to think about how much You love me! You sent Jesus to earth to show us what it looks like to love others. I'm so glad You died to forgive my sins. Now I know Your love, and I want to love You with all my heart in return.

Good night, God!

Amen.

What makes you feel loved by your friends and family?

MY GOAL

No matter how much you want, laziness won't help a bit, but hard wor will reward you with more than enoug

Proverbs 13:4

Proverbs 14:23

Dear Dad in heaven,

Help me not to give up when I am learning new things that are a bit tough.

Help me to be patient with myself even when I make mistakes and have to try many times before I reach my goal.

Good night, God!

Amen.

What is one thing you want to practice more so you can get better at it?

NO STAR IS MISSING

Who created the stars? Who gave them each a name? . . . The Lord is so powerful that none of the stars are ever missing.

Isaiah 40:26

Psalm 147:4

Dear God,
When I make stars with a cookie cutter, I can count them afterward.
But the stars You have created are far too many to count—and you even have a name for each of them!
That's amazing!
Thank You for being so creative and powerful.
Good night, God!
Amen.

What are some of your favorite things that God has created?

His power at work in us can do far more than we dare ask or imagine.

Ephesians 3:20

Genesis 45:4–9

Dear God in heaven,
It's amazing that the same
power that raised Jesus
Christ back to life is living
and working inside of me.
Help me to remember this
when I feel weak and small.
Good night, God!
Amen.

What do you think God
wants to help you do?

I'M NOT ON MY OWN

I will be there to help you wherever you go.

Joshua 1:9

John 10:27–30